# Alphabet
# GARDEN FRIENDS
Letters, Numbers, Colors, and Fun Facts
## - Coloring Book -
by Antonietta Fazio-Johnson

## Copyright Material.
## Thank you for supporting creativity and respecting the work of the artist.

---

Alphabet Garden Friends
ISBN: 978-0-9992802-2-5

Copyright ©2020 IndianWolf Studios LLC
Art and Illustration by Antonietta Fazio-Johnson

All right reserved. No part of this book may be reproduced or transmitted in any form or by any means, electronic or mechanical, including photocopying, recording, or by any information storage retrieval system, without the express written permission of the publisher.

The information provided within this book is for general informational purposes only. While we try to keep the information up-to-date and correct, there are no representations or warranties, express or implied, about the completeness, accuracy, reliability, suitability or availability with respect to the information, products, services, or related graphics contained in this book for any purpose.

IndianWolf Studios LLC
Pittsburgh, Pennsylvania 15216
www.IndianWolfStudios.com
jason.johnson@indianwolfstudios.com
a.johnson@indianwolfstudios.com

Contact IndianWolf Studios LLC at one of the emails above for any inquires about this book.

**36 Single-Sided Illustrations**! So you don't have to choose which image to put up on display!

**Fun Facts!** Learn about garden friends while you color!

**Cutting Guideline.** So that pages can be easily removed, colored, and displayed! (Ask an adult for help.)

Great for colored pencils and crayons.
**Tip:** Some markers may bleed through, so slip something behind the page being colored to prevent possible bleed through.

There is no right or wrong way to color.
Don't be afraid to color outside the lines!
**Be creative and have fun!**

---

Dear Parent / Teacher / Guardian / Coloring Enthusiast,

Hello! Thank you for purchasing my coloring book and supporting creativity!

I am a Pittsburgh based artist, illustrator, designer, and co-owner of IndianWolf Studios, a husband and wife team that creates boardgames, card games, playing cards, and digital games.

The illustrations in this coloring book were inspired by the art I created for our garden themed card game. If you are interested in seeing more of our projects, we welcome you to stop by our website and sign up for our mailing list.

Thank you again!
We are a team of two. Your purchase supports an artist and allows us to continue creating more great books and games. Whether you purchased this for yourself or a friend or child, we thank you and hope it is enjoyed!

Have a wonderful and creative day!
Antonietta

---

Hello Friend,

I am happy that you picked this coloring book to color!

I have always loved to draw and color. That's why I became an artist! I would make art when I was happy and when I was sad. I would even make art to tell stories.

The pictures in this coloring book were so much fun to create! I am excited to share their smiling faces with you here.

Have fun! And remember, it's okay to color outside the lines!

Happy Coloring! (^_^)
Antonietta

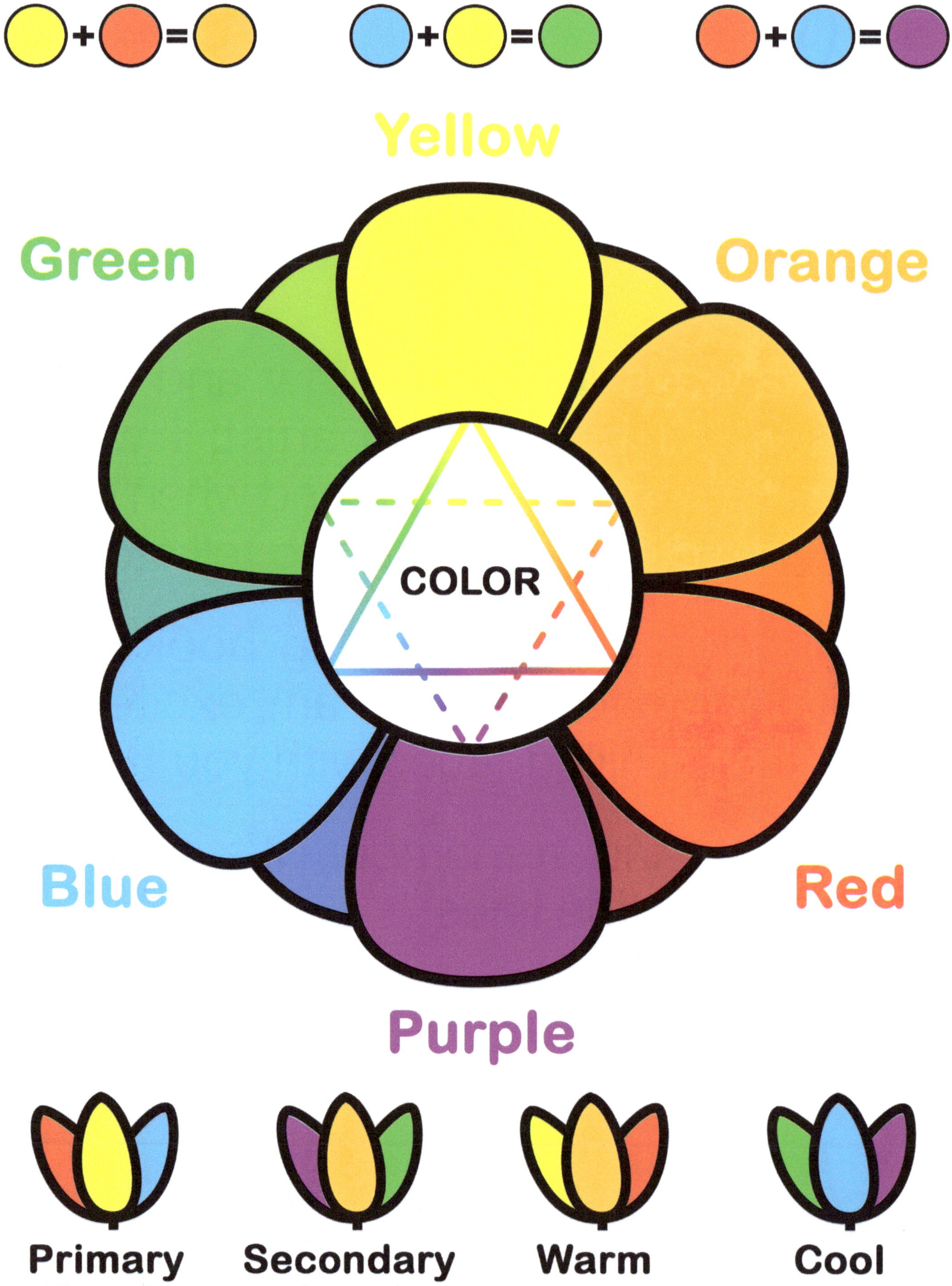

# Yellow

## Green
## Orange

### COLOR

## Blue
## Red

# Purple

**Primary**

**Secondary**

**Warm**

**Cool**

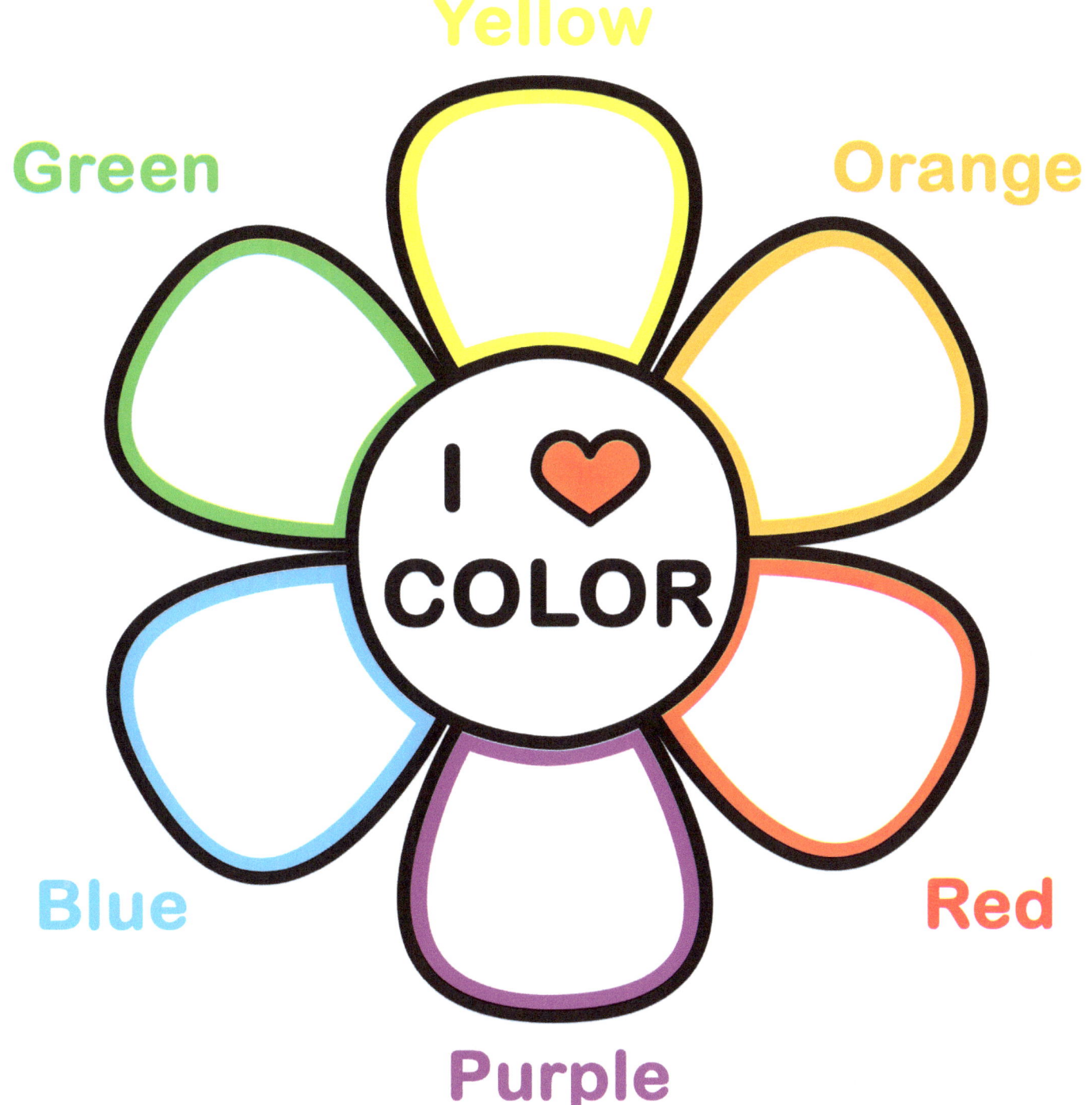

**This book belongs to:**

_____

# Asparagus

Asparagus is a perennial herb.

Perennials grow back every year.

Herb and herbaceous plants have stems that are soft and not woody.

Asparagus have green scale-like leaves and long green stems.

# ASPARAGUS

/    /                                    Colored by:

# Broccoli

Broccoli is part of the cabbage family.

Broccoli have a thick **green** stalk, **silvery-green** leaves, and a large **green** flowering head.

If you let broccoli bloom, it will make a bunch of tiny **yellow** flowers!

There is also **purple** broccoli!

**Purple** broccoli tastes bitter, sweet, and a bit peppery.

# Carrot

Carrots are root vegetables.

Root vegetables grow under the ground.

Many carrots are orange.

There are white, yellow, red, and purple carrots too!

# Deer

Deer are herbivores.

Herbivores only eat plants.

Deer love to eat berries, flowers, and vegetables!

A baby deer is called a fawn.

Fawns are **reddish-brown** with white spots on their back.

When a fawn grows up, its fur turns **greyish-brown** and the spots disappear!

# Eggplant

Also known as an aubergine.

Eggplants are usually **dark purple**.

Eggplants can also be **black**, **white**, or **white** and **purple** striped.

Some eggplants are long and thin. Some are rounder or egg-shaped.

Eggplants make **white** or **purple** flowers.

Eggplants are nightshades. Tomatoes, potatoes, and peppers are nightshades too.

# EGGPLANT

/     /

*Colored by:*

# Flamingo

Flamingos are a type of wading bird.

Flamingos have long necks, long thin legs, and a **black**-tipped beak.

Adult flamingos are light pink to **bright red** in color.

Young flamingos are greyish-red.

Flamingos get their color from the food that they eat!

A plastic flamingo can be a fun garden decoration!

# Grub

Grubs are the larvae
of scarab beetles.

Larvae are insects that have hatched
from an egg and have not yet
changed into their adult form.

Grubs have a plump white body with
a reddish-golden-brown head.

Grubs like to eat the roots
of plants and vegetables.

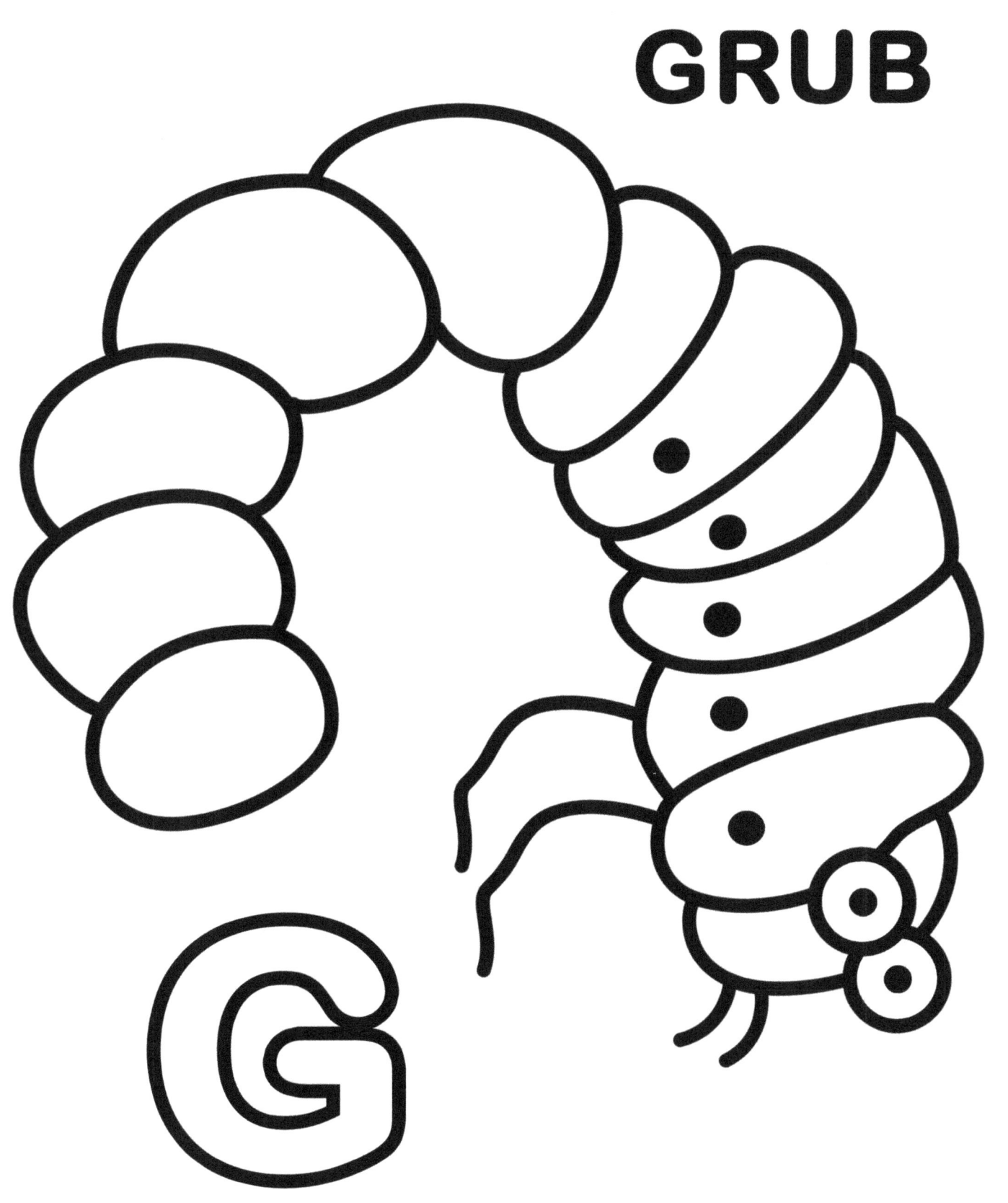

# Honey Bee

Honey bees are **golden-yellow** with **brown** or **black** **bands**.

Honey bees pollinate fruits and vegetables.

Honey bees collect and store nectar from flowers to make honey!

Honey bees need to gather nectar from 2 million flowers to make 1 pound of honey!

The type of flower the honey bee gathers nectar from determines the taste, texture, and smell of the honey.

# HONEY BEE

/       /                                                    Colored by:

# Ice Cream

Ice cream can be a cool treat after a long day of gardening!

Inga edulis, also known as the ice cream bean, is a tropical fruit.

The fruit has a semi-sweet vanilla flavor that tastes like ice cream!

The tree has **white** pom-pom like flowers and the fruit looks like big **green** bean pods.

The pulp inside is sweet and **white** with a chewy cotton-candy like texture. It also has large **green** or **black** seeds.

**ICE CREAM**

/   /  Colored by:

# Jalapeño

A hot **dark green** pepper that can turn **red**, **orange**, or **yellow** when it is ripe.

Peppers are nightshades.

Astronauts like to eat fruits and veggies.

In 1982, jalapeños traveled into space.

Astronauts on the International Space Station even have a "space garden."

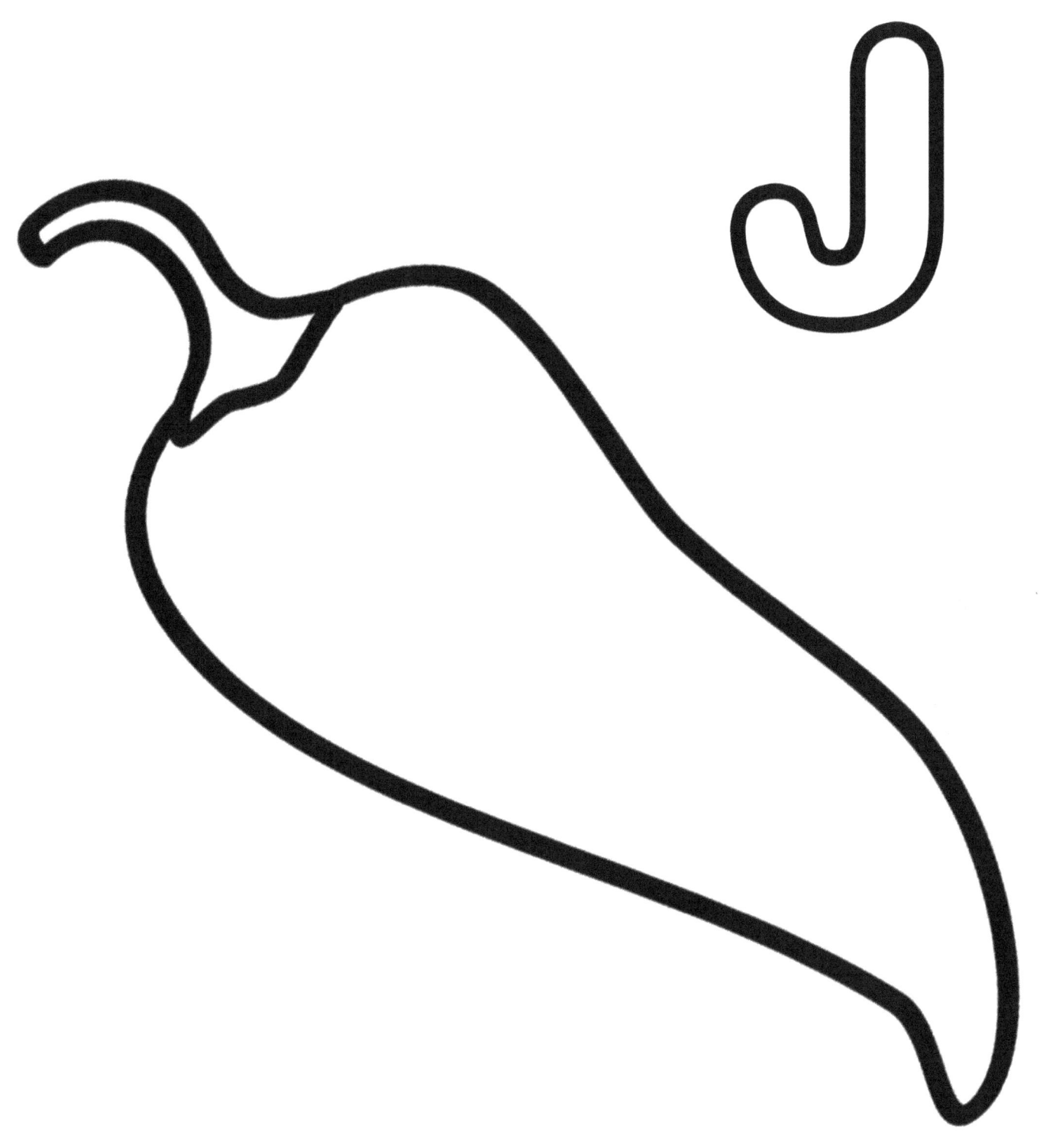

**JALAPEÑO**

/     /     Colored by:

# Kohlrabi

Kohlrabi have **green** leaves and a big bulbous stem that grows above the ground.

Kohlrabi stems can be **light green**, **white**, or **purple**.

Kohlrabi tastes similar to broccoli stems, just a bit sweeter.

# Lettuce

Lettuce can range from **light green** to **dark green**.

Most lettuce are **green**, but some varieties are **reddish-brown**.

The darker the lettuce, the more nutritious!

# LETTUCE

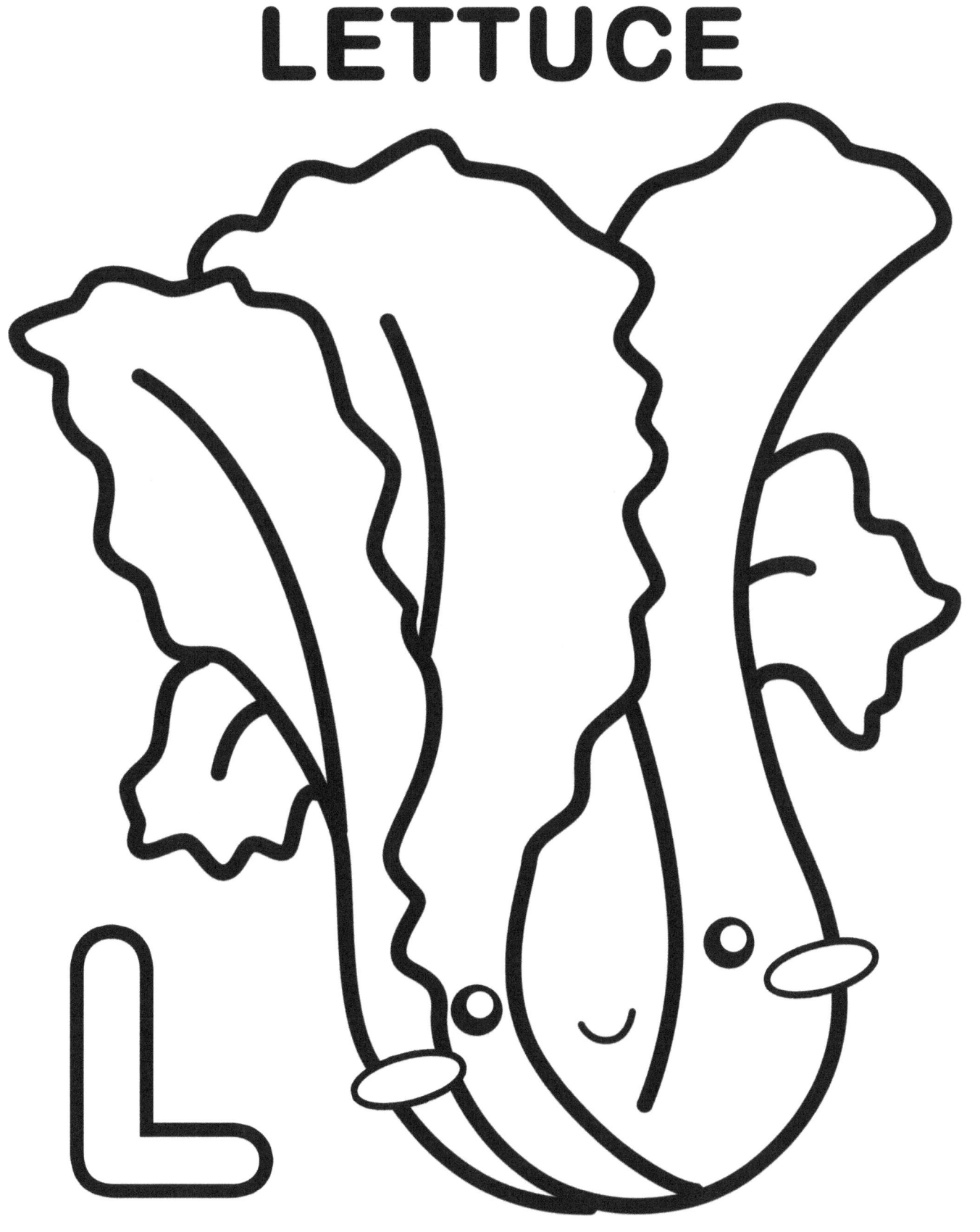

Colored by:

# Mouse

Mice is the plural word for mouse.
One mouse. Two mice.

Mice like to munch on seeds
and vegetables in the garden.

Mice also eat insects and weed seeds.

Mice have big appetites.
A mouse can eat 15 to 20 times a day!

Field mice can be a range of **brown**
colors with a grey or white belly.

A mouse house is called a burrow.
Mice are very tidy and have separate
places in their burrows for storing
food and sleeping.

Alphabet Garden Friends | © 2020 IndianWolf Studios LLC | www.IndianWolfStudios.com

# Nopal

Also called opuntia or prickly pear.

Nopal is a type of edible spiny cactus.

The flat parts are called pads.
The fruits are called prickly pears.

Nopal pads are green.
The fruits can range from green to red.

Nopal pads can be slightly sour, citrusy, lightly bitter, or even tasteless.
The fruit is sweet.

Nopal are crisp on the outside and soft, slimy, slippery, and sticky on the inside.

# N
## NOPAL

/    /     Colored by:

# Onion

Onions are one of the oldest vegetables in the world.

Most onion bulbs are **white**, **yellow**, **purple**, or **red**. Onions make long **green** or **blue-green** tubular leaves.

If left to bloom, onions will make a long stem with a round ball of little **white** flowers.

The heaviest onion weighed over 18 pounds!

# Pinwheel

Pinwheels can be a fun decoration for a garden!

Pinwheels can be any color!

Red, orange, yellow, blue, green, purple, white, black, brown.

Pinwheels spin when they are blown by the wind.

# PINWHEEL

P

_/_ _/_  Colored by:

# Quail

Quail are small, plump, birds that live on the ground.

Some quail are **dark brown** with **brown** and **white** streaks, a **grey-blue** chest, and a **light brown** belly.

Some quail have six overlapping drooping feathers on their head called a plume.

Quail love to eat seeds, grains, berries, and flowers. Sometimes they even eat leaves, roots, and small insects.

Quail lay cute little eggs. The egg shells are **cream**-colored with **brown** speckles and splotches.

Alphabet Garden Friends | © 2020 IndianWolf Studios LLC | www.IndianWolfStudios.com

# Rabbit

Rabbits love to snack on vegetables!

Rabbits can be good for your garden too. They help eat vegetable scraps and make the soil better for planting.

Domesticated rabbits have soft fur that can be many different colors, patterns, and lengths.
**Black**, white, cream, **golden-brown**, light brown, **dark brown**, grey.

Wild rabbits are lean with long thin legs and upright ears.
Wild rabbits have courser, shorter, **grey-brown** or tan flecked fur.

# Sun

Sunlight helps plants grow! Some plants like lots of sunlight and some plants like the shade.

Plants use energy from the sun to turn air and water into food. This is called photosynthesis!

On Earth, the sun looks yellow, orange, or red.

But, the sun is actually white! Because the sun is all the colors of light mixed together.

Rainbows are light from the sun separated into colors!

# Tomato

Tomatoes are a fruit!

Tomatoes are often **red**, but they can also be **green**, **yellow**, **orange**, **pink**, **purple**, **brown**, **black**, or **white**.

Some tomatoes even have **stripes**.

In 1984, as part of a NASA education program, 12.5 million tomato seeds were left in space. 6 years later, the seeds were brought back to Earth and given to children to grow!

# Ugni

Also known as the Chilean guava or strawberry myrtle.

Ugni is a very small fragrant fruit that grows on an evergreen shrub.

Evergreens have leaves that stay green all year.

The shrub has glossy **dark green** leaves and makes white or pale pink bell-shaped flowers.

The berry is red, white, or purple and tastes like a tart strawberry!

# Vanilla

Vanilla is a tropical climbing orchid.

Vanilla plants make long skinny **green** bean pods that are the fruit.

Vanilla fruits are called beans.

Vanilla flavor is made from dried vanilla beans!

When vanilla beans are dried they turn **black**.

Vanilla plants make large **white**, **yellow**, **cream**, or **light green** flowers.

# Watering Can

A great tool for watering your plants and garden.

Plants are made of up to 95 percent water.

Plants need water to make their own food.

Plants absorb water through their roots. The amount of water a plant gets affects how it grows.

Some plants need lots of water and some plants only need a little bit.

Watering cans can be all different shapes, sizes, colors, and materials.

# WATERING CAN

/    /     Colored by:

# Xigua

Pronounced she-gwah.

Also known as a watermelon!

Xigua is a large round or oval fruit.

It has a hard rind that can be **black**, **dark green**, or **light green** and **yellow** striped.

The inside can be **reddish-pink** or **yellow** and has **black** seeds.

Xigua is sweet and watery!

**XIGUA**

# Yam

Yams are perennial herbaceous vines that make starchy root tubers.

Yams have a dry, bark-like, rough, **brown** skin.

Yams can be white, **purple**, **red**, **yellow**, or **pink** on the inside.

True yams are not the same as sweet potatoes.

In the US, sweet potatoes are often called yams.

The "yam" you buy at the grocery store is most likely a sweet potato!

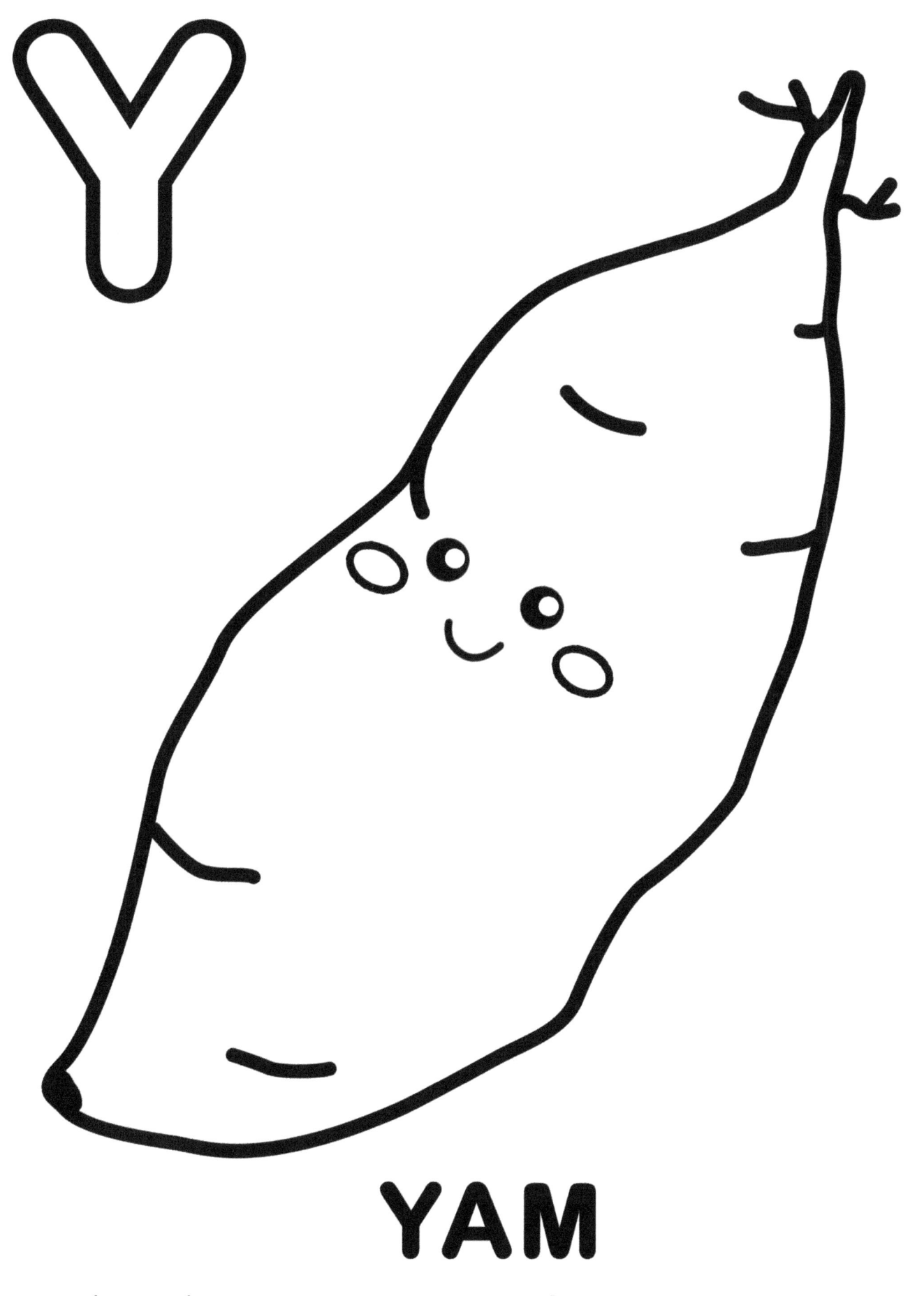

# Zucchini

Also called a courgette.

Zucchini is a summer squash.

Zucchini range in color from **yellow-green** to very **dark green**.

There are also **yellow** or **golden** zucchini. They are not the same as **yellow** squash.

Zucchini make large edible **yellow-orange** flowers.

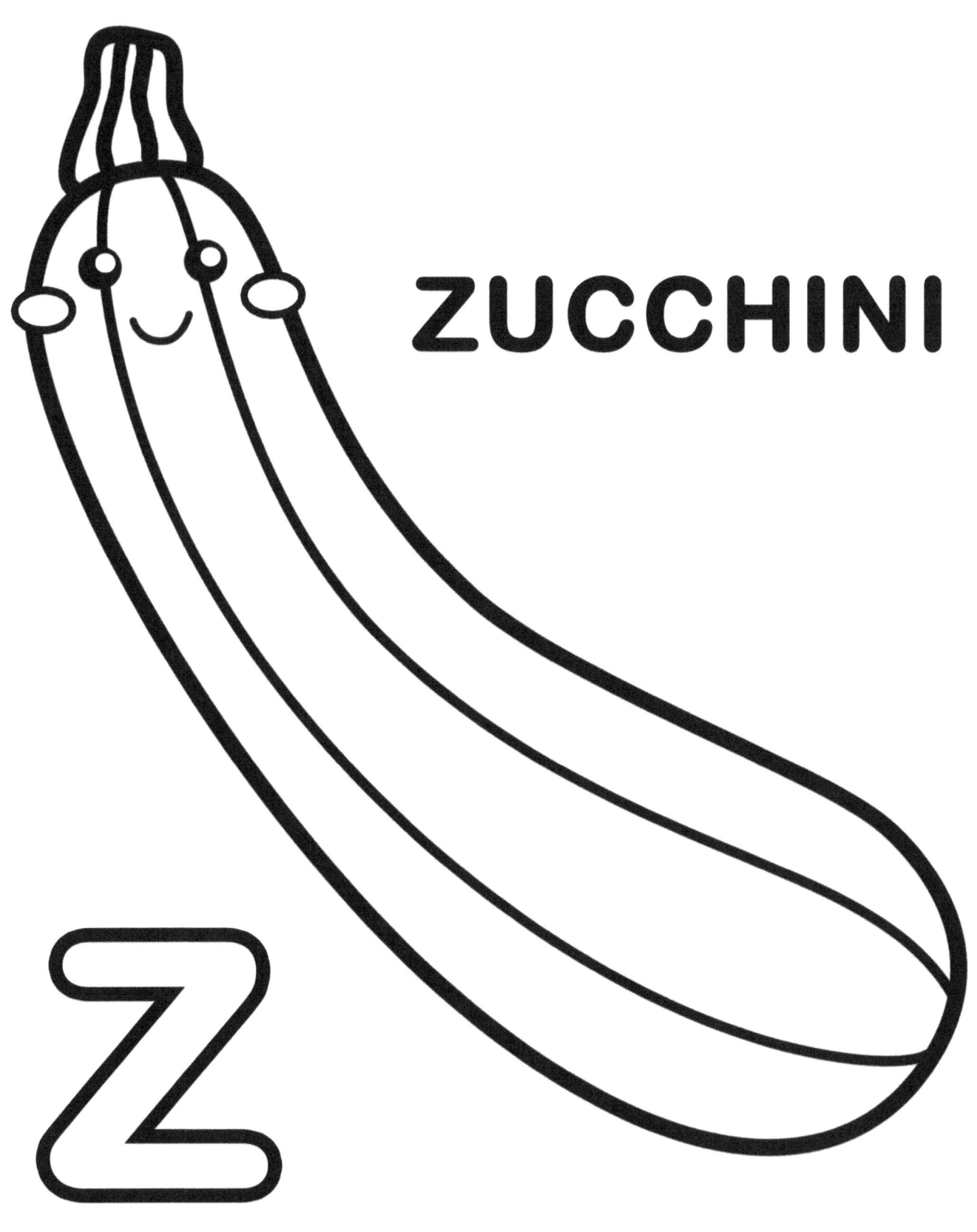

ZUCCHINI

/     /
Colored by:

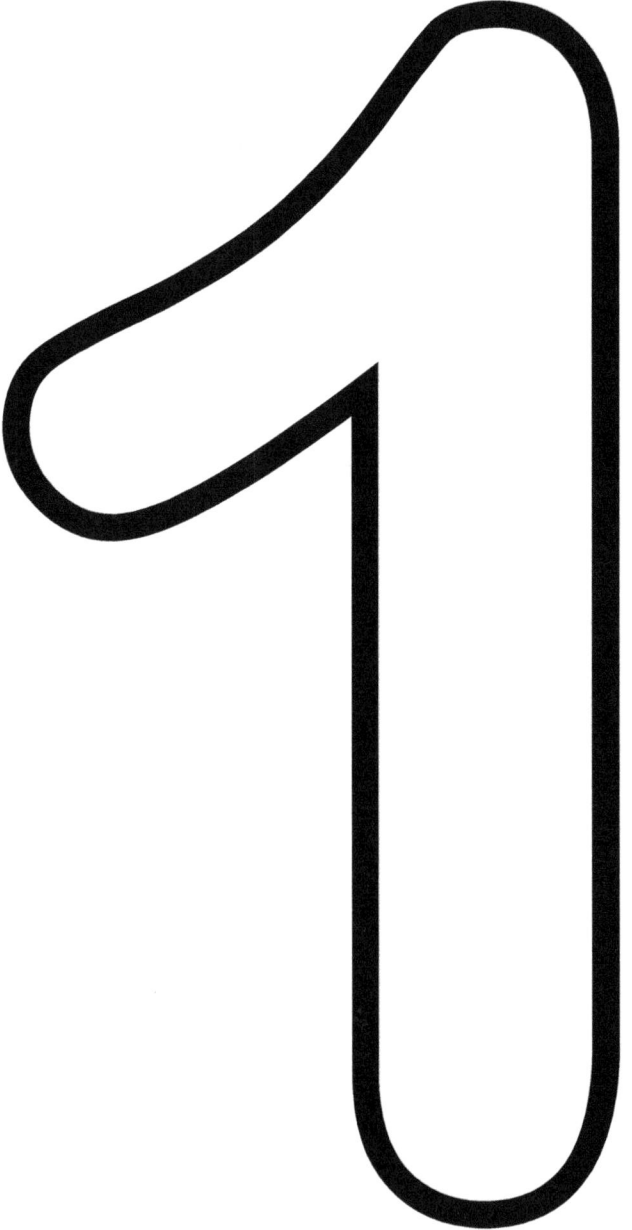

**one raccoon**

/   /   Colored by:

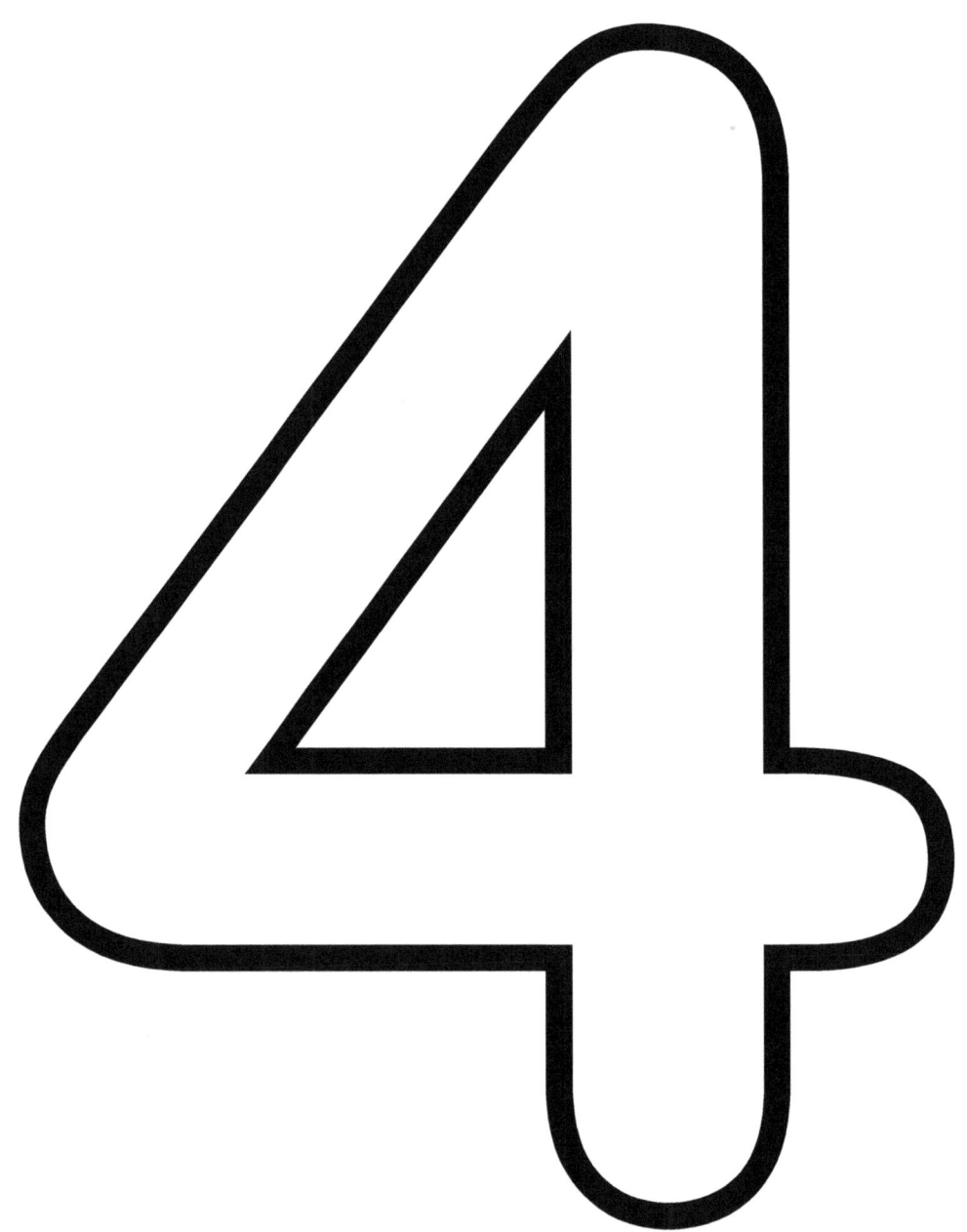

# five strawberries

/    /                              Colored by:

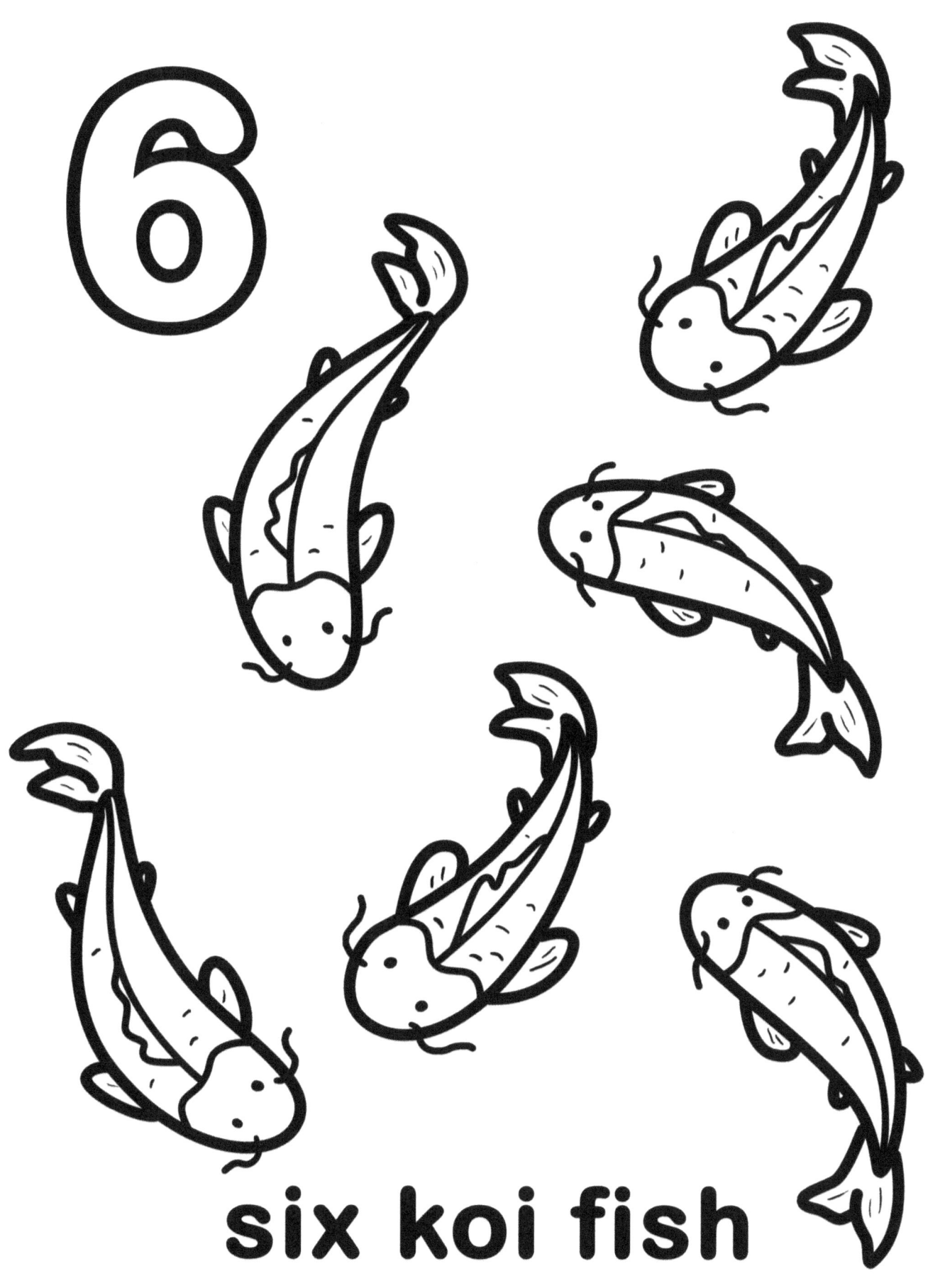

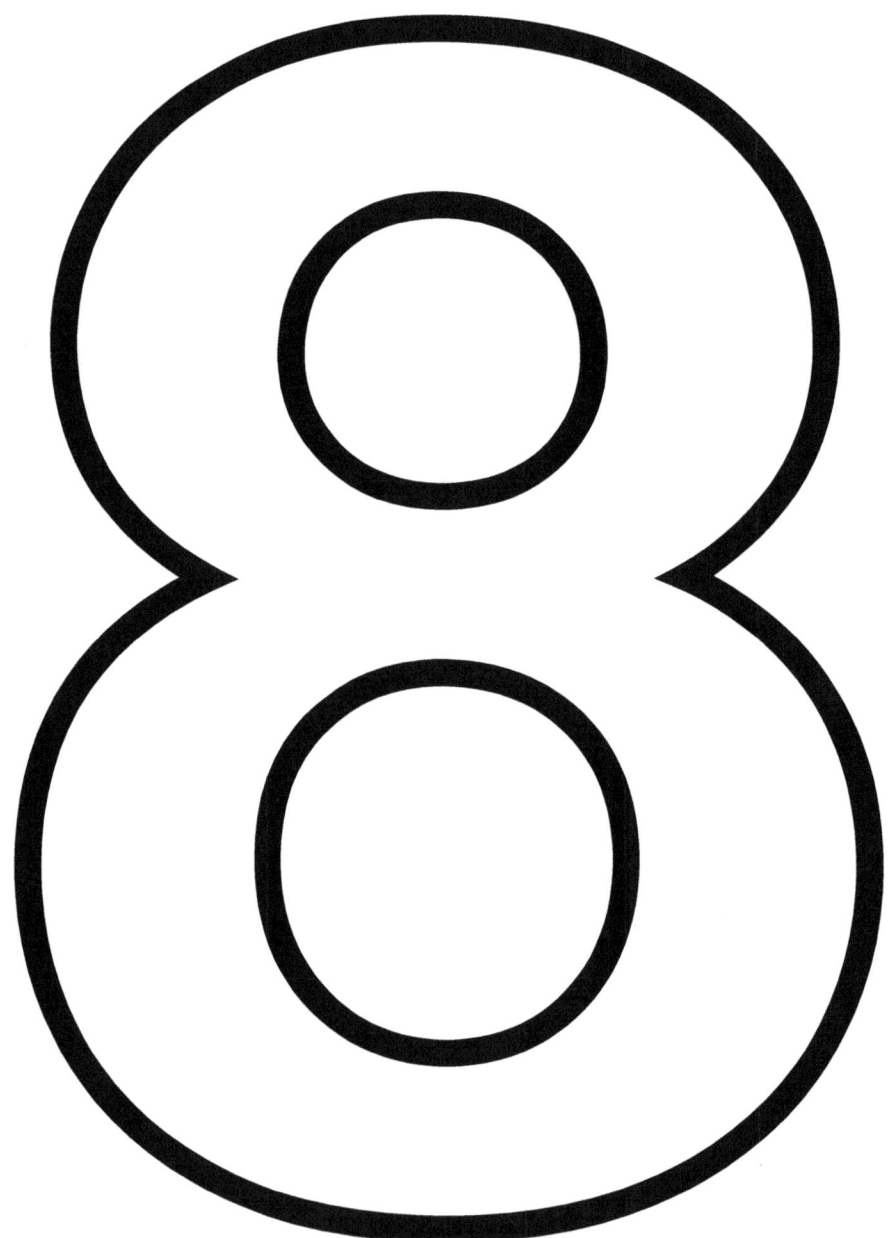

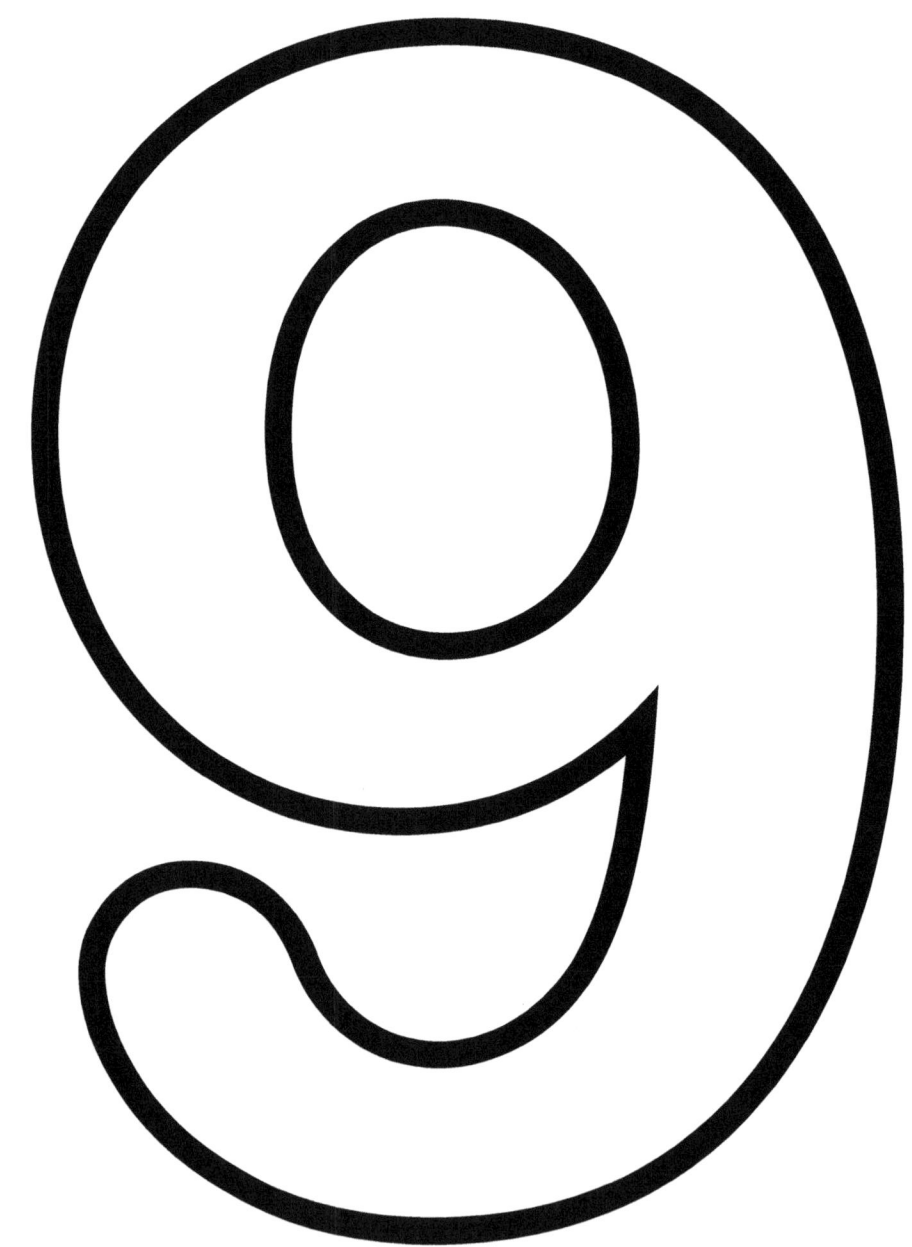

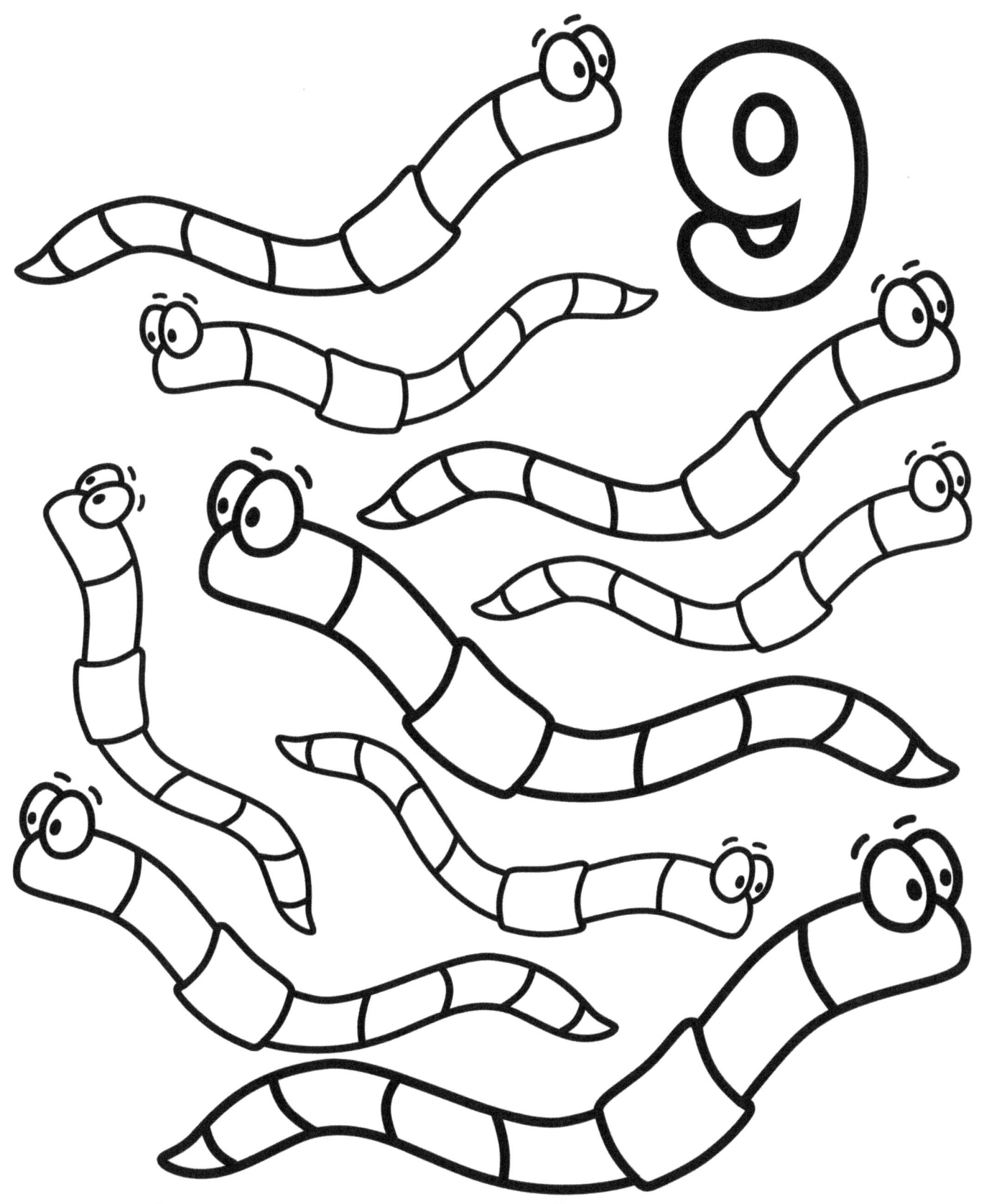

**nine earthworms**

/    /                              Colored by:

You may also like:

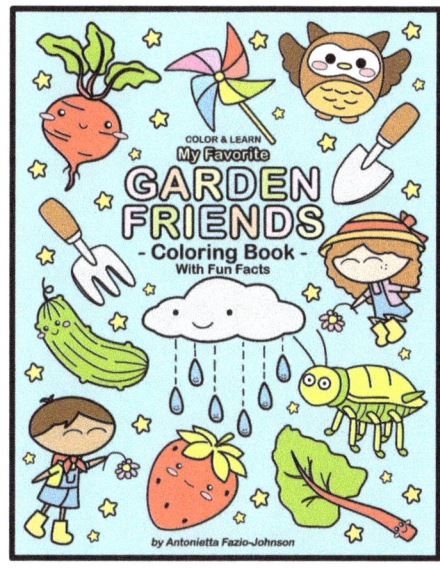 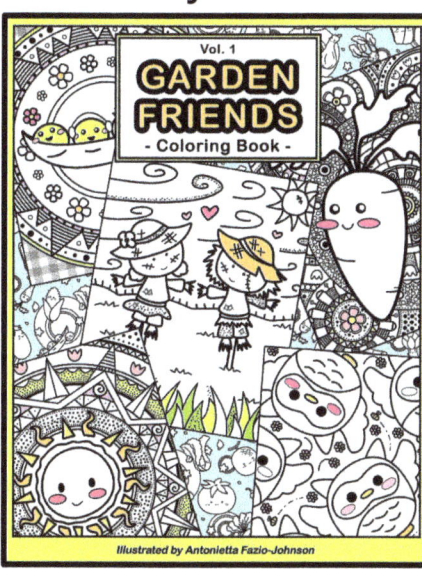 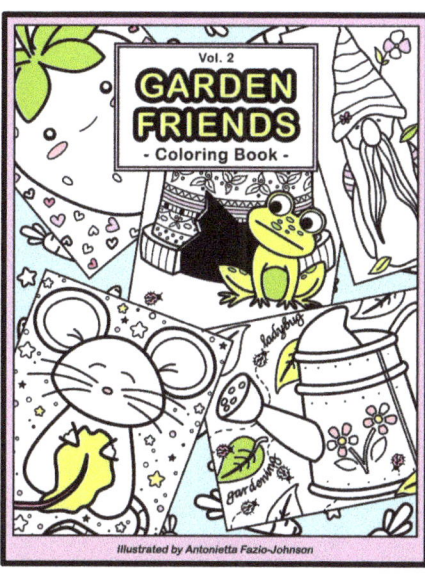

  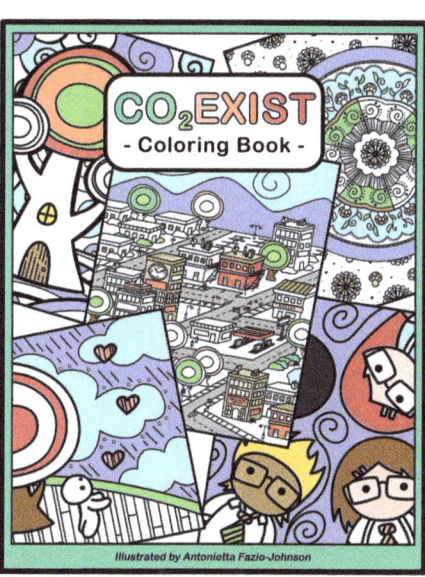

FIND US ONLINE
**www.IndianWolfStudios.com**

FIND US ON FACEBOOK
@IndianWolfStudios

FIND US ON GOODREADS

We love to hear from our fans!
Stop by and let us know if you enjoy your coloring book!
Your review helps bring our work to more people. Thank you!

Questions? Comments?
jason.johnson@indianwolfstudios.com
a.johnson@indianwolfstudios.com

We also make games and playing cards.
Stay up to date on our projects and new releases. Sign up for our mailing list!